JOURNAL

EMDR-inspired techniques designed to help you reset your nervous system and unlock your inner resilience fast.

BY TONI SANDS M.ED., LPC, CIT
EMDRIA CERTIFIED EMDR THERAPIST
&
JACQUE BOW ROUSSELOW M.ED., LPC, LCDC, EMDRIA
APPROVED CONSULTANT

There is so much more to your story.
Healing happens inside your own window of tolerance.
Be on your way with love and light!

—Jacque and Toni

Copyright © 2025 by Brisa Therapeutics
All rights reserved.
ISBN: 979-8-89324-684-1

No part of this book may be reproduced, stored in a retrieval system, or transmitted in any form or by any means—electronic, mechanical, photocopying, recording, or otherwise—without prior written permission of the publisher, except for brief quotations used in reviews or articles.

The opinions expressed by the Author are not necessarily those held by the Publishers.

The information contained within this book is strictly for informational purposes. The material may include information, products, or services by third parties. As such, the Author and Publisher do not assume responsibility or liability for any third-party material or opinions. The publisher is not responsible for websites (or their content) that are not owned by the publisher. Readers are advised to do their own due diligence when it comes to making decisions.

Published by Franklin Publishers

Printed in the United States of America

For permissions, inquiries, or additional copies, contact:

Franklin Publishers

www.franklinpublishers.com

Website Qr Code

Brisa Therapeutics

Our story

Hi! We're Jacque and Toni. We're Licensed Professional Counselors (LPCs) and EMDRIA Certified EMDR Therapists. We are also great friends, moms, and fellow humans.

Our story and journey began as two friends learning how to be therapists in this wide world and, at the same time, navigating our own human experience.

We began our journey as therapists between 2010 and 2016, driven by a shared dream of helping people and making a positive impact on the world. Being a therapist is incredibly rewarding, though it can also be challenging. We've always strived to make a meaningful difference in every life we touch, but of course, that wasn't always possible. At times, we found ourselves feeling like something was missing from our toolboxes as therapists—we just couldn't pinpoint what it was.

Along the way, we were fortunate to receive training in a specialized, evidence-based form of trauma therapy called EMDR

(Eye Movement Desensitization and Reprocessing). Rick Levinson, one of the most renowned EMDR trainers in the world, came to our hometown (thanks to Dee and Cheri!). On top of that, our EMDR consultant and dear mentor, Dee Blinka, was the recipient of the prestigious Francine Shapiro Award in 2017. We were truly privileged to be trained by such wonderfully experienced and exceptional mentors.

From that moment on, we noticed a profound change in our lives—both personally and professionally. The missing link had been found. Becoming EMDR therapists was one of the most meaningful and life-changing experiences we'd encountered up to that point. It remains a transformative and magical experience, not only for us but for our clients as well.

As time went on, we continued to see clients—often back to back—feeling incredibly grateful to accompany them on their journeys of healing and growth. We watched their lives transform in the most remarkable ways. These techniques truly worked. With these tools, we saw the light return to people's lives, a light we knew had to be shared far and wide.

With long waitlists and the often powerless feeling that came when someone couldn't receive the help and support they needed right away—due to various obstacles—we knew we had to take action.

That's when Brisa Therapeutics was born, first in our minds and hearts. Armed with matcha teas, markers, and poster boards, we sat down in Toni's living room and brought Brisa to life—a mental health and wellness program designed to deliver powerful, effective, and affordable healing techniques to everyone.

We have created an entire ecosystem to help:

The Brisa Book Series, Volumes 1-5, The Brisa app, Brisa Courses, and most importantly, a way to carry out our mission of helping the world heal, regulate, and transform using the power of EMDR-inspired protocols along with your own healing power.

How do I use the Brisa Book series?

You are welcome to use the card deck as a guide. When you feel a strong emotion or notice being triggered, the cards can direct you to the recommended chapter or "toolkit." We suggest carrying the card with you to help navigate life's ups and downs.

You can read the books cover to cover or go straight to the protocol you need in the moment. To provide a cohesive experience, we've repeated some introductory paragraphs at the beginning of each protocol so that each chapter stands on its own.

We encourage you to utilize all five volumes. Volume 5, the journal, is designed to help you solidify and deepen your experiences as you work through the tools and techniques.

The Brisa app and courses have audio notes and videos to follow along with.

How many of these words describe how you feel a lot of the time?

- Anxious
- Dysregulated
- Triggered
- Agitated
- Zoned out
- Exhausted

Fearful

Frustrated

Negative body sensations

Negative thoughts

Negative feeling

Distracted

Depressed

Unmotivated

Burned out

... and the list goes on, but this is just to name a few.

We've been there, and we totally get it. Being a human is hard. You are not alone, and we're here to help. We like to say, "We have a toolkit for that!"

Our programs will guide you to tap in (literally) and utilize your own natural, powerful healing mechanisms to rewrite and rewire your mind, body, and spirit.

More info:

As EMDR therapists, we do something called "positive resourcing" before we begin working on the stressful stuff. The process of positive resourcing can last several sessions and strongly continues throughout their therapeutic journey.

It is when and how we help equip our clients with the inner support, skills, and strengths they need to access to be able to process the hard topics.

After engaging in positive resourcing sessions, our clients reported significant improvements in various areas of their lives. They experienced being less triggered, a decrease in trauma responses, reduced negative emotions, lower levels of anxiety, and lifting of depression. Many also noted feeling physically better, more emotionally regulated, experiencing fewer cravings and addictive behaviors, and an overall sense of increased positivity, joy, hopefulness, and capability.

We have been using these powerful healing techniques in our own lives and with our clients since 2016, and we can confidently say that they have transformed lives. The positive impact these techniques create is often beyond words.

We also understand that not everyone can access help exactly when they need it, and that's where Brisa comes in. Brisa is here to lead and guide you through tough times in the moment, offering the support and tools you need to navigate life's challenges.

Go with love and light.

"Your situation is hard, and you can do hard things!"

-Jacque and Toni

Dedicated to all of those who forged the way, shared with us your wisdom, compassionate approaches, and so graciously taught us the art of healing. We are forever grateful. Because of you, we are able to share these gifts with the world.

-Jacque and Toni

Internal Retreat:

What vivid sights do you see in your internal retreat?

Imagine your internal retreat, focusing on engaging all your senses and providing detailed descriptions. Remember, this is an exercise in visualization and imagination to promote relaxation and well-being.

_____
_____
_____
_____
_____
_____

What textures and surfaces can you touch or feel?

For example, soft, velvety grass beneath your feet as you walk barefoot, lying on a comfortable chaise lounge, wrapped in a soft warm blanket, or resting against a smooth sturdy tree trunk. These are just a few examples to inspire your guided imagery. Allow your imagination to create vivid sensory experiences as you envision the various tactile sensations that enhance your internal retreat.

_____
_____
_____
_____
_____
_____

What sounds do you hear in this serene space?

For example, the gentle breeze rustling through tall grass or swaying trees, the distant sound of waves crashing against the shore, tranquil melodies of wind chimes, or a cozy warm crackling fire. Allow your imagery to transport you to your internal retreat, where the sounds bring you a sense of peace, relaxation, and tranquility.

_____

_____

_____

_____

_____

What distinct aromas or scents fill the air?

For example, the invigorating scent of a nearby ocean or sea breeze, the calming and grounding aroma of sandalwood or patchouli, the soothing scent of a crackling fireplace, or the sweet and earthy scent of freshly fallen rain. Allow your imagination to create vivid sensory experiences as you envision the various delightful aromas that enhance your internal retreat.

_____

_____

_____

_____

_____

What tastes linger on your palate?

For example, imagining the taste of a freshly cut pineapple or piece of ripe watermelon, enjoying a cup of aromatic, freshly brewed coffee or tea, or maybe you taste a tangy and refreshing raspberry sorbet. Notice any tastes that bring you comfort to enhance your experience in your internal retreat.

_____
_____
_____
_____
_____
_____

What emotions are associated with this space and what positive emotional state do you commonly experience when you are there?

Important note: If the emotions linked to the place you've chosen start to feel overwhelming or distressing, it's advisable to discontinue the exercise and return to the audio to create an alternate internal retreat. This new retreat should be designed to elicit feelings of calmness and positivity.

_____
_____
_____
_____
_____
_____

What word or words best capture the essence or essence of this place?

When it comes to creating a special name for your internal retreat, it's essential to choose something that resonates with you and evokes a sense of calmness and peace. The key is to select a name that encapsulates the essence of your internal retreat and helps guide you towards a state of calm and positivity.

_____
_____
_____
_____
_____

In your Internal retreat, if this place could impart wisdom or provide a supportive pep talk, what encouraging messages would it offer?

These messages serve as reminders of your inner strength, the importance of self-compassion, embracing growth, and cherishing the present moment. They encourage you to believe in yourself and pursue your dreams while providing comfort and guidance along the journey.

_____
_____
_____
_____

During each visit to your internal retreat, do you observe any new or previously unnoticed aspects?

Take a moment to recognize something new and refreshing that you have recently discovered within your internal retreat. If you haven't noticed any changes, that's absolutely okay! However, you might observe an intensified vibrancy or a strengthening of positive emotions.

_____
_____
_____
_____
_____

What do you appreciate most about this space?

For example, the tranquility experienced, solitude, safety, sense of strength, connection with self, or reflection and growth. Remember, the aspects appreciated about an internal retreat can vary from person to person, as it is a deeply personal experience influenced by individual preferences, needs, and desires.

_____
_____
_____
_____
_____

Can you think of another activity or place in your life that elicits a similar sense of emotional or sensory experience as the one described earlier?

For example, walking in nature or hiking, relaxing on a beach or by water, dancing or engaging in physical exercise, creating art or writing, spending time with loved ones, or attending concerts or live performances. Remember, what elicits certain feelings or sensations can differ based on personal interests, past experiences, and individual preferences.

_____
_____
_____
_____
_____
_____

In what situations or instances would you find it beneficial to utilize this exercise for enhancing your overall well-being?

It is recommended to practice these techniques regularly, especially during moments of stress or anxiety, to cultivate a grounded state and promote a sense of presence and well-being.

_____
_____
_____
_____

How did the addition of deep breathing techniques and bilateral stimulation make you feel during this exercise?

_____
_____
_____
_____

On a scale of 0 to 10, with 0 representing a fine or neutral state and 10 indicating the worst possible condition, what number would you assign before starting this exercise?

_____
_____
_____
_____

What was your number at the end of the exercise?

What changes or improvements have you noticed, if any, in yourself or your experiences? Look for little glimpses of your positive future self in your daily life.

_____
_____
_____
_____

Nature's Treasures:

Let's explore and connect with the elements. Where will you be doing this exercise?

You're welcome to engage in this exercise outdoors or in a space that allows you to establish a connection with the elements, whether it's through direct experience or visual imagery.

_____
_____
_____
_____
_____
_____
_____

What sights do you see in your environment?

Take a moment to observe your surroundings and fully immerse yourself in the experience.

_____
_____
_____
_____
_____
_____

What auditory experiences do you notice?

For example, do you hear the sound of flowing water, chirping birds, crackling fire, or gentle raindrops? Be specific.

_____
_____
_____
_____
_____
_____
_____

What emotions do you perceive and observe in your body during this experience?

For example, calmness, joy, gratitude, serenity, or contentment. Emotions can vary from person to person, and everyone's emotional experiences are unique.

_____
_____
_____
_____
_____
_____
_____

What scents or aromas do you detect in your environment?

For example, you might notice the invigorating scent of rain as it fills the air, the earthy aroma of fresh cut grass as you walk through a park, or the briny scent of the ocean as you stand near the shoreline. These scents can evoke specific emotions and sensations within your body, such as a feeling of freshness, rejuvenation, or a connection to nature.

_____
_____
_____
_____
_____
_____
_____

What textures and surfaces can you touch or feel?

_____
_____
_____
_____
_____
_____

What tastes do you notice? Are you experiencing any salivation or the ability to generate saliva in your mouth?

Salivation, apart from its role in digestion, can also have a cognitive impact by helping to keep us present and focused. The act of salivating activates the parasympathetic nervous system, which is responsible for promoting a calm and relaxed state. This can aid in grounding us in the present moment, enhancing mindfulness, and reducing stress or anxiety.

_____

_____

_____

_____

_____

When you establish a connection with the elements, what observations or sensations do you notice in your body?

Note what sensations and observations you experience when your feet make contact with the earth, you take a deep breath outside, or connect with water. How does your body feel as a result?

_____

_____

_____

_____

_____

Can you recall a positive experience of connecting with the earth beneath your feet?

For example, you might experience the sensation of cool water gently flowing over your feet as you walk barefoot through a babbling stream. You might feel the softness of grass beneath your toes as you stroll across a lush, green lawn. Alternatively, you could perceive the sensation of tiny pebbles or sand shifting beneath your feet as you explore the shoreline of a peaceful lake. These textures can elicit feelings of grounding, relaxation, and a connection to nature.

_____
_____
_____
_____

What are some grounding techniques that have been found effective in anchoring yourself to the present moment and maintaining a grounded state?

For example, deep breathing, body scanning, sensory grounding, mindful observation, grounding with movement, grounding affirmations, or visualization. Remember that different grounding techniques work for different individuals, so it's essential to explore and find what resonates with you.

_____
_____
_____
_____

In what situations or instances would you find it beneficial to utilize this exercise for enhancing your overall well-being?

It is recommended to practice these techniques regularly, especially during moments of stress or anxiety, to cultivate a grounded state and promote a sense of presence and well-being.

_____
_____
_____
_____
_____
_____
_____

How did the addition of deep breathing techniques and bilateral stimulation make you feel during this exercise?

_____
_____
_____
_____
_____
_____
_____

On a scale of 0 to 10, with 0 representing a fine or neutral state and 10 indicating the worst possible condition, what number would you assign before starting this exercise?

_____
_____
_____
_____
_____
_____

What was your number at the end of the exercise?

What changes or improvements have you noticed, if any, in yourself or your experiences? Look for little glimpses of your positive future self in your daily life.

_____
_____
_____
_____
_____
_____

Paper Boats:

To engage your imagination, vividly describe your water source, and share the color it appears to be?

_____
_____
_____
_____

If you're open to reflection, what did you choose to send off in your paper boat?

Take a moment to observe your surroundings and fully immerse yourself in the experience. Please feel free to be open and provide as much information as needed or keep your response brief, whichever you prefer.

_____
_____
_____
_____

When you released your boats, how did it make you feel in that moment?

_____
_____
_____
_____

What positive intention did you hold during this experience?

A positive intention is typically framed in a positive language, emphasizing what you want to invite, create, or cultivate in your life. It serves as a guiding principle to help you navigate challenges and make decisions.

_____
_____
_____
_____
_____

How does your positive intention make you feel?

_____
_____
_____
_____
_____

What notable differences did you observe or experience when sailing your positive intentions compared to the heavier issues?

_____
_____
_____
_____

In as much detail as possible, what is the description of your container?

___

Where did you choose to store your container, ensuring it is safe, secure, and located at a distance from you?

___

How did it feel when you left your container? Did you notice a difference, if any, with distance?

___

Afterward, which calm or pleasant place did you visit, and how did you arrive there?

_____

_____

_____

_____

Why do you think you chose this method of transport?

_____

_____

_____

Can you think of another activity or place that elicits a similar positive emotion to what you experienced in this context?

For example, walking in nature or hiking, relaxing on a beach or by water, dancing or engaging in physical exercise, creating art or writing, spending time with loved ones, or attending concerts or live performances. Remember, what elicits certain feelings or sensations can differ based on personal interests, past experiences, and individual preferences.

_____

_____

_____

_____

We hope you're enjoying your journal! This journal is designed to enrich your experience and further enhance your success, after utilizing the Brisa Books, 1-4.

We are so glad you're here!

Inner Parts:

What inner part of self do you call on to help support you?

_____
_____
_____
_____
_____

What external support do you call on?

_____
_____
_____
_____
_____

What objects off comfort or support strength? (Examples: blanket, suit of armor, outter bubble of protection, map, shield, 12-foot tall teddy bear, powerful crystal, etc.)

_____
_____
_____
_____

What words of encouragement do your inner team provide to you?

_____
_____
_____
_____
_____

How do you feel different when you call on your inner team or supportive self?

_____
_____
_____
_____
_____
_____

What activities help you feel this same way?

_____
_____
_____
_____

Write down a positive memory that involves you accessing your inner strengths:

_____
_____
_____
_____
_____
_____
_____
_____
_____

What job(s) does your inner team have? (Examples: To protect, provide guidance, nurturing, humor, abundance, wisdom, etc.)

_____
_____
_____
_____
_____
_____
_____
_____

Draw a sketch representation of your inner team:

After you draw, take a few moments to tap and breath as you look at your sketch

What are some instances that you might utilize this meditation to improve your well-being?

_____

_____

_____

_____

_____

Name something new that you noticed about your inner team that you hadn't noticed before:

_____

_____

_____

_____

_____

How did adding in deep breathing techniques and bilateral stimulation effect your body and the meditation?

_____

_____

_____

_____

_____

What was your number before you began the meditation (0 is fine, 10 is the worst)?

_____

_____

What was your number at the end of the meditation?

_____

_____

Look for little glimpses of this in your dailylife. Call in your inner team anytime you need or want to!

Go with love and light!

Ride the Wave:

When strong emotions arise, what are your typical responses or strategies for dealing with them?

How would you characterize or describe the nature of the strong emotion you are experiencing?

What are some constructive and positive physical outlets or activities that allow you to channel and release the energy generated by a strong emotion?

Engaging in physical activities like running, walking, cycling, working out, dancing, cleaning, and gardening can help release and shift emotional states. Allowing yourself to experience these natural responses, including shedding tears, can contribute to stress release and promote a sense of emotional well-being.

After successfully pushing through and riding the wave of intense emotions, how do you feel? What are the sensations, emotions, or shifts in your state of being that you experience as a result of navigating and embracing the wave of emotions?

_____
_____
_____
_____
_____
_____
_____
_____

If you were to visualize or represent the release of the strong emotions you have experienced, what picture or image comes to mind?

Describe how you would depict the process of letting go and releasing those emotions in a visual form.

_____
_____
_____
_____
_____
_____

How do you recognize or determine that you have effectively shifted through the strong emotions or successfully released them?

Note what indicators or signs you notice within yourself that indicate a sense of resolution or emotional release.

_____
_____
_____
_____
_____

What specific healthy activity do you often find reliably effective in helping you feel better?

For example, walking in nature or hiking, relaxing on a beach or by water, dancing or engaging in physical exercise, creating art or writing, spending time with loved ones, or attending concerts or live performances. Remember, what elicits certain feelings or sensations can differ based on personal interests, past experiences, and individual preferences.

_____
_____
_____
_____
_____

How do you notice a difference in how you feel when you allow yourself to ride the wave of emotions versus when you suppress, bottle up, or avoid feeling those emotions?

_____
_____
_____
_____
_____
_____
_____

In what situations or instances would you find it beneficial to utilize this exercise for enhancing your overall well-being?

It is recommended to practice these techniques regularly, especially during moments of stress or anxiety, to cultivate a grounded state and promote a sense of presence and well-being.

_____
_____
_____
_____
_____
_____
_____

How did the addition of deep breathing techniques and bilateral stimulation make you feel during this exercise?

_____
_____
_____
_____

On a scale of 0 to 10, with 0 representing a fine or neutral state and 10 indicating the worst possible condition, what number would you assign before starting this exercise?

_____
_____
_____
_____

What was your number at the end of the exercise?

What changes or improvements have you noticed, if any, in yourself or your experiences? Look for little glimpses of your positive future self in your daily life.

_____
_____
_____
_____

A River Flows:

When strong emotions arise, what are your typical responses or actions? How do you typically navigate and handle these intense emotional experiences?

Take note of whether these ways are helpful or not helpful for you. Observe how they impact your well-being and make a note of their effectiveness.

_____
_____
_____
_____
_____

After successfully envisioning and allowing yourself to let it flow, how do you feel?

Reflect on how this experience was different from what you would typically do in similar situations. Notice any changes or variations in your approach and compare it to your usual behaviors and note emotional or physical sensations you experience as a result of this release.

_____
_____
_____
_____
_____

What supportive and encouraging words or messages emerged for you during this experience?

As you notice the shift and release, pay attention to any supportive words that come to mind or how your body feels different. Take note of any positive messages or sensations that arise during this process.

_____
_____
_____
_____
_____

What other positive ways can you channel and release the energy of strong emotions? How can you engage in activities that allow you to express and redirect that emotional energy constructively?

Engaging in physical activities like running, walking, cycling, working out, dancing, cleaning, and gardening can help release and shift emotional states. Allowing yourself to experience these natural responses, including shedding tears, can contribute to stress release and promote a sense of emotional well-being.

_____
_____
_____
_____
_____

How do you feel different when you allow the flow versus when you stuff, bottle, push down, or try to avoid feeling it?

Pay attention to any shifts you notice in your body. It could be a feeling of lightness, calmness, or any other physical sensations that indicate a positive change.

_____
_____
_____
_____
_____
_____

What internal changes do you observe when the strong emotions begin to dissipate or release?

Pay attention to any shifts you notice in your body. It could be a feeling of lightness, calmness, or any other physical sensations that indicate a positive change. Take note of these shifts and acknowledge the positive impact they have on your well-being.

_____
_____
_____
_____
_____
_____

What intention do you want to set for yourself going forward?

Setting an intention means consciously identifying and stating a specific focus or desired outcome for a particular situation or period of time. An example of setting an intention is, "My intention is to embrace challenges as opportunities for growth and learning."

_____

_____

_____

_____

_____

In what situations or circumstances do you envision using this exercise as a means to enhance your overall well-being?

It is recommended to practice these techniques regularly, especially during moments of stress or anxiety, to cultivate a grounded state and promote a sense of presence and well-being.

_____

_____

_____

_____

_____

How did the addition of deep breathing techniques and bilateral stimulation make you feel during this exercise?

_____
_____
_____
_____

On a scale of 0 to 10, with 0 representing a fine or neutral state and 10 indicating the worst possible condition, what number would you assign before starting this exercise?

_____
_____
_____
_____

What was your number at the end of the exercise?

What changes or improvements have you noticed, if any, in yourself or your experiences?

_____
_____
_____
_____

Becoming:

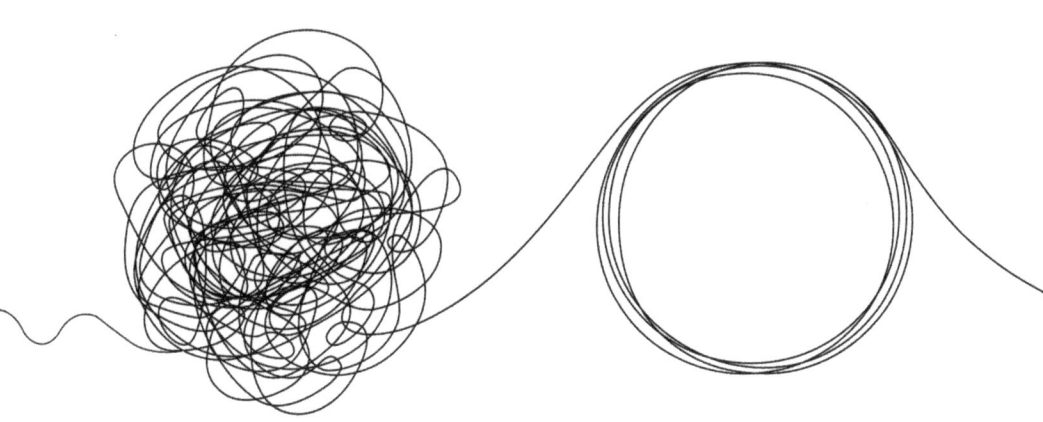

When you imagine your future self and your desired life, please provide a detailed description of what you envision?

Paint a vivid picture, including specific details and aspects that are meaningful to you. Remember, the details and aspects that make this picture meaningful to you are unique and personal.

_____
_____
_____
_____
_____
_____

When you envision your future, what activities and actions do you see yourself engaging in?

For example, pursuing a fulfilling career, traveling and exploring the world, building and maintaining meaningful relationships, engaging in hobbies and personal interests, making a positive impact, or enjoying a healthy lifestyle.

_____
_____
_____
_____
_____

When you envision your future self and desired life, how would you describe the emotions and inner feelings that you experience?

_____

_____

_____

_____

_____

In your envisioned future self and desired life, how do you perceive yourself presenting or expressing yourself to the world?

For example, you may see yourself or present as more authentic, creative, active, leading, sharing and offering knowledge or talents, or collaborating with others. It's important to note that these are just a few examples, and individuals may have unique perceptions of how they want to present or express themselves based on their values, passions, and aspirations.

_____

_____

_____

_____

_____

_____

_____

_____

When you access and envision your future template self, what noticeable differences do you observe or experience in yourself?

Imagine the multi-sensory experience as you draw your desired future self into your life and manifest it. Allow yourself to dream big and envision all the details noting specific changes or shifts in your thoughts, behaviors, or overall demeanor. Also, cultivating a practice of gratitude for this aspect of yourself can also be helpful and empowering.

_____
_____
_____
_____
_____

If you were able to connect with this aspect of yourself more frequently, how do you think things would shift or be different in your life? What changes or transformations do you envision occurring as a result of strengthening this connection?

When you imagine and connect with this part of yourself, remember to engage all your senses. Visualize, hear, feel, smell, and taste the experience vividly in your imagination. Use the power of sensory imagination to enhance the richness and depth of your vision.

_____
_____
_____
_____

Is there an activity or a specific place in your life that elicits a similar feeling or sensation to what you've just imagined?

For example, walking in nature or hiking, relaxing on a beach or by water, dancing or engaging in physical exercise, creating art or writing, spending time with loved ones, or attending concerts or live performances. What elicits certain feelings or sensations can differ based on personal interests, past experiences, and individual preferences.

_____

_____

_____

_____

_____

_____

What word or words best capture the essence or qualities associated with your future template self?

For example, "Knowledgeable," or "Resilient and adaptable."

_____

_____

_____

_____

_____

When you envision the positive and strong part of yourself, what encouraging words or inner pep talk would that part of yourself offer to uplift and motivate you? What words come to the forefront as you imagine this supportive self-talk?

_____
_____
_____
_____
_____

In what situations or circumstances do you envision using this exercise as a means to enhance your overall well-being?

For example, challenging situations, goal setting and achievement, public speaking or presentations, high-pressure environments, leadership and decision-making, overcoming fears and self-limiting beliefs, or networking and social interactions. Tailor the exercise to align with your specific goals and intentions, and let it empower you in any circumstance where you want to show up as your most powerful self.

_____
_____
_____
_____
_____

How did the addition of deep breathing techniques and bilateral stimulation make you feel during this exercise?

Note changes or effects you noticed in your state of mind or body as a result of utilizing these techniques.

_____
_____
_____
_____
_____
_____
_____

On a scale of 0 to 10, with 0 representing a fine or neutral state and 10 indicating the worst possible condition, what number would you assign before starting this exercise?

_____
_____
_____
_____
_____
_____
_____

What was your number at the end of the exercise?

What changes or improvements have you noticed, if any, in yourself or your experiences? Look for little glimpses of your positive future self in your daily life. You can, and you are, becoming.

_____

_____

_____

_____

_____

_____

_____

_____

Addictive Behaviors:

What are some of the specific triggers or situations that tend to lead you towards addictive behaviors?

Allow yourself to explore your thoughts and emotions honestly and seek professional support if needed from the provided links at the beginning of the exercise.

___

___

___

___

___

___

What positive emotion do you associate or perceive as being linked with the addictive behavior in question?

The emotions experienced may be deceptive or misleading positive emotions or feelings that people may experience during addiction (e.g., freedom, emotional numbing, escape, confidence, etc.) that can hinder personal growth, and perpetuate a cycle of dependency.

___

___

___

___

___

___

What are some healthy and authentic ways to cultivate the desired positive emotional state, but without relying on addictive behaviors?

For example, exercise or physical activity, practicing mindfulness and meditation, cultivating positive relationships, pursuing hobbies and interests, practicing and positive affirmations, or seeking professional support when needed. It's important to remember that what works for one person may not work for another. It's about finding what resonates with you and aligns with your values and preferences.

_____

_____

_____

_____

_____

If you were able to replace the addictive behavior with the desired positive behavior, how would your life be transformed?

Note what changes and improvements you envision in various aspects of your life as a result of this shift.

_____

_____

_____

_____

_____

What are some positive physical methods you can employ to effectively shift from a strong craving and also release energy in a constructive way?

Engaging in physical activities like running, walking, cycling, working out, dancing, cleaning, and gardening can help release and shift emotional states. Allowing yourself to experience these natural responses, can contribute to stress release and promote a sense of emotional well-being.

_____
_____
_____
_____

After successfully pushing through a craving, shifting your state, and reaching the other side, how do you feel?

Note what emotions or sensations you experience as a result of overcoming the craving and transitioning to a more empowered state.

_____
_____
_____
_____

How do you envision the release of the energy associated with the craving?

Note what images or ideas come to mind when you imagine the process of letting go and allowing the energy to dissipate or shift.

_____
_____
_____
_____
_____
_____

What are some activities that you find personally effective in improving your mood and overall well-being?

Engaging in physical exercise, walking a pet, practicing mindfulness or meditation, and connecting with loved ones or engaging in social activities are some examples of activities that can help promote a sense of well-being and improve mood.

_____
_____
_____
_____
_____
_____

If you were to receive a positive message from the universe, providing support for your personal journey, what would you envision that message saying?

These messages are meant to provide encouragement, inspiration, and a sense of support during times of difficulty or self-doubt. For example, "You are stronger than you realize. Keep pushing forward," or "Take one step at a time. Progress is made through small, consistent actions."

_____
_____
_____
_____
_____
_____

Are you noticing any changes in the intensity and/or frequency of cravings and usage?

In the upcoming days and weeks, consider tracking your behaviors and cravings.

_____
_____
_____
_____
_____

What fears or obstacles do you anticipate facing on your recovery journey? How can you develop strategies to overcome them?

For example, Obstacle: Negative self-talk and self-doubt. Strategy: Practice self-compassion and challenge negative thoughts with positive affirmations and realistic perspectives. Engage in positive self-talk and focus on your progress and accomplishments. Surround yourself with supportive and encouraging people who believe in your recovery journey.

_____
_____
_____
_____
_____

What are some situations in which you might utilize this exercise to improve your well-being and reduce cravings?

It is recommended to practice these techniques regularly, especially during moments of stress or anxiety, to cultivate a grounded state and promote a sense of presence and well-being.

_____
_____
_____
_____
_____

On a scale of 0 to 10, with 0 being no craving at all and 10 being an intense craving, how would you rate your current craving?

_____
_____
_____
_____
_____

What was your number at the end of the exercise?

What changes or improvements have you noticed, if any, in yourself or your experiences?

_____
_____
_____
_____
_____
_____
_____

Unpain the Brain:

When you experience pain, what are your typical responses or actions?

Note how you instinctively or habitually tend to cope with or address the sensation of pain. Allow yourself to explore your thoughts and emotions honestly, and seek professional support if needed.

_____

_____

_____

_____

What distinguishes clean pain, where you purely observe and acknowledge the physical sensation of pain, from convoluted pain, which involves additional layers of interpretation, meaning, or emotional reactions intertwined with the physical pain signal?

Note what sets clean pain apart is the pure and direct experience of physical discomfort without the additional elements that often accompany it, such as thoughts, fears, negative emotions, and other psychological reactions that can amplify or complicate the pain experience.

_____

_____

_____

_____

_____

Which specific part of your body did you identify and access as your pain-free zone or a space where you experienced relief from pain?

Consider any specific area within your body, from your earlobe to your pinky toe.

_____
_____
_____
_____
_____
_____
_____

In the space you identified as your pain-free zone, what color did you associate with that area?

_____
_____
_____
_____
_____
_____
_____
_____
_____

When envisioning the release of the pain and energy you were experiencing, how did you visualize or imagine this process?

Note what images or representations came to mind as you imagined the release and dissipation of the pain and energy from your body.

_____
_____
_____
_____
_____
_____
_____

After experiencing the release of pain and energy, how do you feel? Did you observe any noticeable shifts in your physical sensations, emotions, or overall state of being?

_____
_____
_____
_____
_____
_____
_____

When you engage in the "Unpain the Brain" exercise compared to when you attempt to stuff, bottle up, push down, or avoid the feeling of pain, do you notice a difference in how you feel?

Note any distinct changes or shifts in your emotional state, mental well-being, or overall experience between these two approaches.

_____
_____
_____
_____
_____
_____

What internal message or sensation do you receive or experience that serves as a signal to you that you have successfully released or diminished the pain?

Note if there is a specific message, feeling, or shift in your perception that indicates a sense of relief or reduction in pain.

_____
_____
_____
_____
_____
_____

Reflect on any lessons or insights you have gained through your journey of pain management. What strategies or techniques have proven helpful for you? How can you build upon these successes?

_____
_____
_____
_____
_____
_____
_____
_____

What differences or changes do you notice when you are leaving the Soul Spa?

_____
_____
_____
_____
_____
_____
_____
_____

In what situations or circumstances can you envision using this exercise to enhance your overall well-being?

Embracing these practices as a part of your holistic wellness regimen to nurture your mind, body, and spirit and to support you in navigating life's challenges with greater resilience and grace.

_____
_____
_____
_____
_____
_____
_____

On a scale of 0 to 10, with 0 representing a fine or neutral state and 10 indicating the worst possible condition, what number would you assign before starting this exercise?

_____
_____
_____
_____
_____
_____

What was your number at the end of the exercise?

What changes or improvements have you noticed, if any, in yourself or your experiences? Look for little glimpses of your positive future self in your daily life.

_____
_____
_____
_____
_____
_____
_____

The Soul Spa:

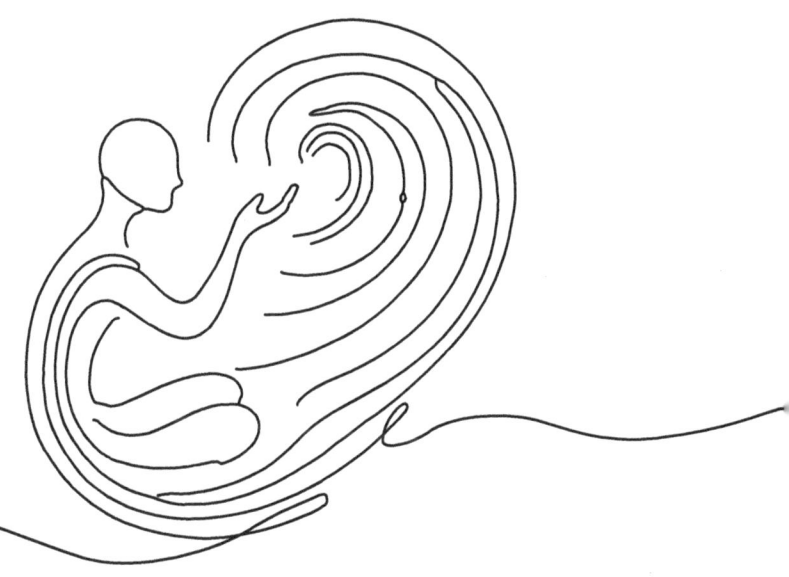

As you set off on your journey to the Soul Spa, what intention did you establish for yourself to guide and uplift you along the way?

To set an intention means to consciously and purposefully identify a specific focus or desired outcome for your thoughts, actions, or experiences. Setting an intention can help guide your mindset, actions, and choices in alignment with your goals, values, or aspirations and serves as a compass or guiding principle.

_____

_____

_____

_____

When you step into the Soul Spa, how would you describe the emotions and sensations that arise within you?

For example, a sense of calmness and peace washes over you, you feel embraced by a warm and welcoming energy, tension and worries melt away as you settle into the soothing ambiance, or a renewed vitality and energy begin to flow through your body. The purpose of a Soul Spa is to provide a space for self-care, relaxation, and rejuvenation, where one can tap into their inner essence and cultivate a deep sense of well-being and connection.

_____

_____

_____

_____

_____

What aspects of yourself or areas in your life do you desire to be restored, rebalanced, and rejuvenated within the Soul Spa experience?

___

When considering your physical body, how would you like to feel and experience it? What specific sensations or qualities do you aspire to cultivate within your physical self?

For example, are you seeking a sense of strength, vitality, and flexibility? Are you aiming for a feeling of balance, ease, and comfort in your body? Is it a sense of grace, agility, and coordination? Or are you seeking a deep connection with your body and a feeling of being fully present in each moment?

___

When contemplating your mind, how would you like to feel and experience it?

Note how you would like to envision experiencing your thoughts and the ways in which you perceive the world around you.

_____
_____
_____
_____
_____
_____

How would you describe your vision of your spiritual self? What qualities, beliefs, or experiences do you envision encompassing your spiritual being?

Please note that spirituality is subjective and can differ among individuals, as it is shaped by unique experiences, values, and cultural backgrounds. It is a personal journey that promotes well-being and a deeper understanding of oneself and the world.

_____
_____
_____
_____
_____
_____

When you take a moment to reflect on your water source from the Soul Spa, what images or visions come to mind? How do you visually perceive this water source in your imagination?

_____
_____
_____
_____
_____
_____
_____
_____
_____

What are some things or aspects of your life that you feel grateful for or find gratitude in?

_____
_____
_____
_____
_____
_____
_____
_____

What "I am" statement or intention would you like to set to guide you as you prepare for sleep?

Using "I am" statements in intention setting can be a powerful practice to help shift your focus, strengthen your self-image, and create a sense of alignment between your conscious and subconscious mind.

_____
_____
_____
_____
_____
_____

What differences or changes do you notice when you are leaving the Soul Spa?

_____
_____
_____
_____
_____
_____

Upon departing from the Soul Spa, what differences or transformations do you observe or experience within yourself? What notable changes have you noticed as you emerge from this rejuvenating space?

_____
_____
_____
_____
_____
_____

In what situations or circumstances can you envision using this exercise to enhance your overall well-being?

Embracing these practices as a part of your holistic wellness regimen to nurture your mind, body, and spirit and to support you in navigating life's challenges with greater resilience and grace.

_____
_____
_____
_____
_____
_____
_____

On a scale of 0 to 10, with 0 representing a fine or neutral state and 10 indicating the worst possible condition, what number would you assign before starting this exercise?

_____
_____
_____
_____
_____
_____
_____
_____

What was your number at the end of the exercise?

What changes or improvements have you noticed, if any, in yourself or your experiences? Look for little glimpses of your positive future self in your daily life.

_____
_____
_____
_____
_____
_____
_____

Vibing:

When you are in a state of high vibrational energy or "vibing," what aspect of yourself feels most present and alive?

Note what emotions or feelings you typically experience during these moments of elevated energy and positive resonance.

_____

_____

_____

_____

When you experience a positive vibe or feel-good emotions, what colors do you associate with these uplifting feelings?

Note what hues or shades come to mind when you envision the visual representation of this positive energy.

_____

_____

_____

When do you find yourself feeling your absolute best?

Note what situations, activities, or circumstances you typically experience a heightened sense of well-being, joy, and fulfillment.

_____

_____

_____

What aspects, qualities, or experiences would you like to invite and cultivate more of in your life?

Note what you aspire to bring forth and nurture in order to enhance your overall well-being and happiness.

_____

_____

_____

_____

_____

_____

When you are in a state of feeling good and vibrating positively, what aspects of your life or experiences do you feel grateful for?

During these moments of positivity and well-being, note of the things, people, animals, places, or circumstances that you appreciate and feel gratitude towards.

_____

_____

_____

_____

_____

_____

When experiencing positive sensations, where in your body do you notice these feelings most prominently or distinctly?

Take a moment to reflect on the specific areas or parts of your body that seem to be the focal point or source of these positive sensations. For example, a warm, glowing sensation emanating from your heart center, a lightness and clarity in your mind, or a soft, comforting feeling in your hands. By becoming aware of these focal points, you can deepen your connection with your body and harness the power of positive sensations for your overall well-being.

_____

_____

_____

_____

How would you describe the differences or shifts that you are noticing between the times when you are feeling positive and the times when you are not?

Note the noticeable contrasts in your thoughts, emotions, physical sensations, or overall state of being.

_____

_____

_____

_____

Do you have a specific mantra or affirmation that you associate with this positive state or that resonates with the experience of feeling good? If so, what is your chosen mantra, and what does it signify or represent for you?

A mantra is a repeated word, phrase, or sound that is used as a form of affirmation or meditation. It is a powerful tool for focusing the mind, cultivating positive beliefs, and promoting a sense of calm and clarity. Examples of mantras include phrases like "I am enough," "I embrace change," or "I radiate love and compassion."

_____
_____
_____
_____
_____

What intention do you wish to set for yourself as you move forward into the rest of your day, week, or weekend that aligns with your desired state of being or the qualities you wish to embody?

Setting an intention means consciously identifying and stating a specific focus or desired outcome for a particular situation or period of time. An example of setting an intention is, "My intention is to embrace challenges as opportunities for growth and learning."

_____
_____
_____
_____
_____

Energy Restoration:

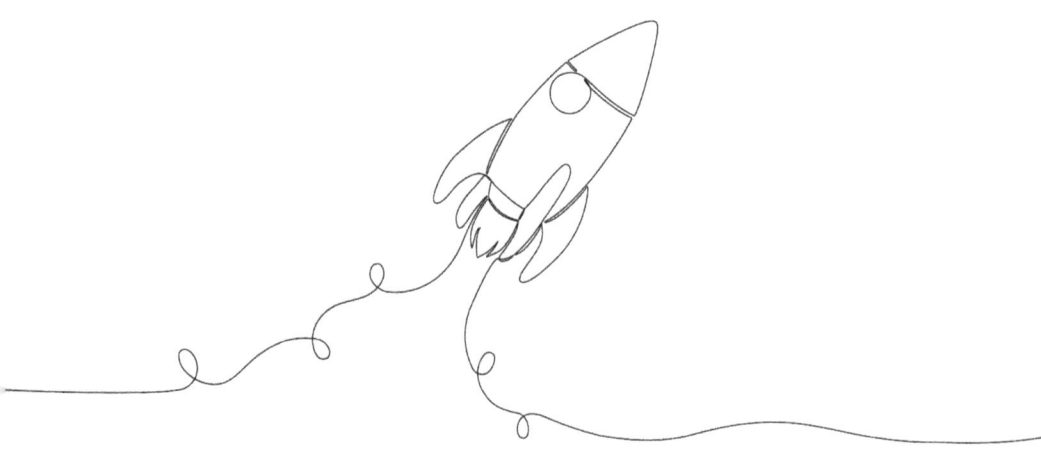

Before we begin, please take a moment to reflect on some offered sleep hygiene tips. Simply note which ones you would like to strengthen?

1. Maintain a consistent sleep schedule
2. Create a sleep-friendly environment
3. Establish a relaxing bedtime routine
4. Limit exposure to electronic devices before bed
5. Manage your daytime habits

___
___
___
___
___

How can you modify or improve these aspects of your sleep hygiene to enhance your overall sleep experience?

These tips may not work overnight, and it may take time to develop a consistent sleep routine. If sleep problems persist, it's recommended to consult a healthcare professional for further guidance and evaluation.

___
___
___
___
___

What is your pre-sleep routine, if any? How do they affect your ability to fall asleep and stay asleep?

___

How do you wind down mentally before sleep? Are there any cognitive or mindfulness techniques you can employ to calm your mind?

___

How does your sleep environment contribute to the quality of your sleep? Are there any changes you can make to improve it?

_____
_____
_____
_____
_____
_____

What are the benefits of following the sun for optimal sleep?

For example, incorporating habits like waking up with the sun, seeking sunlight exposure during the day, and beginning to relax and unwind as the sun sets can be beneficial for your well-being if your schedule permits.

_____
_____
_____
_____
_____
_____
_____
_____

Are there any specific activities or habits (such as screen time, caffeine intake, exercise) that you notice impact your sleep negatively or positively?

Scientifically speaking, it is important to be mindful of consuming caffeine in the late afternoon, evening, and night to support restful sleep.

_____
_____
_____

Are there any medications, substances, or dietary choices that you think might be affecting your sleep? How can you address or modify them?

Reminder, drugs, certain medications, and alcohol can negatively impact your sleep hygiene.

_____
_____
_____

What is one actionable change you can initiate to promote a healthy nighttime routine?

Please refer to sleep hygiene tips if you are unsure.

_____
_____
_____

What are some mindful strategies or actions you can implement to build and strengthen your sleep routine?

_____
_____
_____
_____
_____
_____
_____
_____

What is your level of physical activity during the day? How does exercise or lack thereof influence your sleep quality?

_____
_____
_____
_____
_____
_____
_____
_____

In what situations or circumstances do you envision using this exercise as a means to enhance your overall well-being?

It is recommended to practice these techniques regularly, especially during moments of distress, to cultivate a grounded state and promote a sense of presence and well-being.

_____
_____
_____
_____
_____
_____
_____
_____

How did the addition of deep breathing techniques and bilateral stimulation make you feel during this exercise?

_____
_____
_____
_____
_____
_____
_____

On a scale of 0 to 10, with 0 representing a fine or neutral state and 10 indicating the worst possible condition, what number would you assign before starting this exercise?

___

___

___

___

___

___

What was your number at the end of the exercise?

What changes or improvements have you noticed, if any, in yourself or your experiences? Look for little glimpses of your positive future self in your daily life.

___

___

___

___

___

___

___

___

Disclaimer

This publication does not provide medical advice, diagnosis, or treatment. The content is for educational and informational purposes only. The creators are Licensed Professional Counselors acting as educators in this environment and are not medical doctors. This publication is not intended to replace professional medical advice, diagnosis, treatment, therapy, or therapeutic support. Always consult a medical professional regarding any medical issues or symptoms you may be experiencing, and before beginning any new wellness regimen. If you are experiencing a medical or mental health emergency, please call 911 or go to your nearest medical facility. Never disregard medical or mental health advice because of something you read or hear in this publication.

This program may not best for everyone- including people with Complex PTSD or certain Disociative Disorders. Please check with your medical and or mental health provider before using any new program. This program is for educational purposes and teaches self administered wellness and coping techniques. They are designed for coping and regulation. I understand there are risks associated with any wellness program involving health. If at any point you feel worse, please discontinue the educational techniques and contact your mental health and or medical provider. By continuing with this program, you are hereby giving your informed consent and taking responsibility for proceeding. Brisa Therapeutics LLC is not responsible for personal issues experienced.

To learn more or find an EMDR therapist, visit:
www.emdria.org

ABOUT THE AUTHOR

Jacqueline Rousselow

Toni Sands

Jacque and Toni are Licensed Professional Counselors and EMDR Certified Therapists. At the time of this publication, they have a combined 25 years of experience as therapists. They co-founded Brisa Therapeutics, an interactive mental health and wellness app and book series in 2021.

Jacque and Toni share a deep life long friendship, as well as the mission to help bring healing and joy to the world. Both Jacque and Toni have a true love for the desert, where they raise their families. They share the passion of learning, teaching and helping others heal.

www.ingramcontent.com/pod-product-compliance
Lightning Source LLC
Chambersburg PA
CBHW050727010526
44107CB00009B/771